Ursula Andkjær Ols

THIRD-MILLEN

Translated by Katrine Øg

MW00573621

ACTIONBOOKS

The third-millennium heart is a
place of many chambers

complex being with bridges and passages
transporting bodies around
increasingly fleeting and flexible patterns

castle that

humans, animals, gods
work, loneliness
babel and ivory

move through.

My outwardly face: I wash it in whatever
streams by.

WHAT STREAMS IS MATERIAL AND IMMATERIAL

Cannot keep it solid, the material = random = uncontrollable
liquid, rushing like rivers through the immaterial
landscape. Whatever is streaming streams too fast;
a suction occurs, a hollow feeling of being *mise en abyme*
thrown into a fractal abyss. Whatever is streaming only
streams to stream on, never reaching its destination.
Then four walls of unreality are erected: a room
in which I can sit completely motionless and escape.

The material = necessary = determined, static, solid. The immaterial
runs through a solid reality like natural springs, and the eyes recover
their moisture. I cannot move: the material creates four walls of
density, while dreams walk over my contact area with
their life-giving yellow, blue and green.

MY NAME IS WAITING ROOM

Namedrunk, nameless, I rub these categories
against each other: thus fire was created.

I am warm while you are freezing: thus fire was created.

I have names, I have a
well in my forehead and nothing to cover it with:
thus fire was created.

My name is Everything, so that when you call my name, everything will happen.

Like a current interpretation of an original hypothesis
I form my own meaning of content:
Hands of God.

My name is Nothing, so that when you call 1000 names I will come
no matter what, I will come.

Everything will be thick and RED, everything will flow.

My name is Waiting Room
my eyes, my lungs are named Waiting Room
my heart

with atrium, ventricle, cubicle
complex being

is named Waiting Room

it all comes and goes, everything flows.

I handle my pain
like an adult human being, I do nothing.
I sit here, I have a view, I do nothing.

All vessels are connected.

.

I am the fence that fences the nameless, the reservation, the universe, my distant interior.

I can visit as often as I want.
Nobody can visit me.

His name is Rain On Chapped Lips
his cobalt clothes are named Rain On Chapped Lips
the land he walks on, the way he is tall and thin, like a blade
over humans, is named Cobalt Rain On Chapped
Words. His words fall like Cobalt Rain:

"Le monde occidental est perverti. Pas les individus. La culture est
pervertie, pas l'individu." *
(Hawad)

I wash my hands, neck and face
outwardly; I let the moon touch what cannot (must)
cannot (must) be inside the

atrium, ventricle, cubicle

of the heartspace.

Their name is Inevitable
their wife and husband with yellow eyes are named Inevitable
their children with half faces named Inevitable
their single-chamber house and their country named Inevitable
their dog, their clothes, their voiceless vermin named Inevitable
their name
their name
their vengeance is Inevitable.

Life does not mean the same to them as it does to us.
Life never means the same. Cannot (must).

Their name is Nameless
their wordless speech is named Nameless
their husband named Nameless
their wife, their children named Nameless
their house, their chamberless heart named Nameless
incapable of beating;
their reappearance will be Nameless.

I ornament myself with
abysses painted on my forehead like a quality-conscious pig.

I lie on *their* sweat-embroidery.

My name is Harmless
what I do is called Harmless
what I drink every morning called Harmless
what I eat every evening called Harmless.

I wish to be tall and black and grave; I need it.
My destructions are already countless.

I take my name from my surroundings: a place so namedrunk it
matches the namedrunk in me.

I name the place after myself: a place so nameless it
matches the nameless in me.

We walk around with our distant interior, throwing
out light. O to be beautiful when the fire erupts.

My name is Waiting Room.

I am allowed to be upset here.
I have to be upset here.
I cannot get out of here until I've been upset.

Not a center: a waiting room.

The heart is a trivial place that things stream through.

You, I have used (without your knowledge) to label myself
as what I am: your invisible servant.

I have used you, my invisible creature, to label myself as
what I am: Everything and Nothing.

I am indebted to you, servant, when I label myself as visible,
namedrunk, Everything.

I have used Nothing to call myself what I am, servant, so that
when you call my name, everything will happen.

I am indebted to you, invisible creature, when I call myself Everything
without your knowledge, without my knowledge
so that when you call my name.

I have used you, without your knowledge, to call myself
Nothing, so that when you call 1000 names, I will come, I will come.

You are in debt to me for naming yourself, for what you are
my invisible servant. We are connected like this: chained, so that
when you call *your* name, *I* will come.

Let us love so that when I call, your name will grow and fill up everything.

Let us love so that when you call, my name will.

Does the wave fear its dissipation, or does it feel itself as everything?

THE WORLD IS BABEL AND IVORY

I rub a desert of correlation against a desert of change:
thus fire was created. Then I rub a desert of necessity against
a desert of coincidence, until

correlation = coincidence
change = necessity
closeness = closeness

NAMEDRUNK/NAMELESS

You have a name, even though you haven't seen the light of day
you have a name, even though you'll never see the light of day.

That is the structure.

Your name is possible, even though you've never existed:
you are namedrunk/nameless.

That is the structure, continued.

The fact that loss is a defeat; that every
loss is connected to RED and smeared
in RED no matter how well you carry it.

You I have lost, it was like a defeat
and you I have lost, it was like a defeat.

Everything I have been pregnant with
and lost is a defeat smeared in RED
and counting.

It sounded like my heart was beating outside of me; as if someone was walking
up the stairs, dragging their feet on the steps. Thought someone was there,
walking up the stairs, dragging their feet on the steps: it was my
exoheart, turning everyone into siblings, beating into me
from the outside. You always belong
to more than one place.

All vessels are connected.

When I lie on my back and cry, tears run from my temples and into each ear canal. When the pressure is high enough, the fluid is pushed back into my tear ducts and I can lie like this, a closed orbit, mute jubilation, fountain, for several thousand years.

Unclear: who's imitating who
The moon in my sink. I wash
my hands in the moon, wash neck and face
outwardly, in the moon
unclear, question: Who's washing who?
The water is no longer clear

my hands are

It's smooth here: a hand can stroke.

And in the egg there was a fixture
and in the fixture sat the chromosomes
and in the chromosomes lay the hypothesis.

It's smooth: here, you can paint
a longing with
RED.

And in the garden there was a bush
and in the bush there was a nest
and in the nest there was an egg
and in the egg there was green grass
and death.

First I got used to pains as big as teacups.

Then I got used to pains as big as mill wheels.

Then I got used to pains as big as

towers
and at the end of the towers there are spires
and at the end of the spires there is a sky tied up with strings of gold and steel
and at the end of the sky tied up with strings of gold and steel there is

you, caressing my body while I do the work of suppression.

Namedrunk/nameless

There was a tree in the middle of the woods, the prettiest tree ever seen
and the green grass grows all around.

And in this tree there was a bed, the prettiest bed ever seen
the bed in the tree and the tree in the woods
and the green grass grows all around.

And in this bed there was an apple, the prettiest apple ever seen
the apple in the bed and the bed in the tree and the tree in the woods
and the green grass grows all around.

And on this apple there was a forehead, the prettiest forehead ever seen
the forehead on the apple and the apple in the bed
and the bed in the tree and the tree in the woods
and the green grass grows all around.

And in this forehead there was a well, the prettiest well ever seen
a well in the forehead and the forehead on the apple and the apple in the bed
and the bed in the tree and the tree in the woods
and the green grass grows all around.

And in the well a small leaf fell, the prettiest leaf ever seen
the leaf in the well and the well in the forehead and the forehead on the apple
and the apple in the bed and the bed in the tree and the tree in the woods
and the green grass grows all around.

And on this leaf there was a nest, the prettiest nest ever seen
the nest on the leaf and the leaf in the well and the well in the forehead
and the forehead on the apple and the apple in the bed
and the bed in the tree and the tree in the woods
and the green grass grows all around.

And in this nest there was an egg, the prettiest egg ever seen
the egg in the nest and the nest on the leaf and the leaf in the well
and the well in the forehead and the forehead on the apple
and the apple in the bed and the bed in the tree and the tree in the woods
and the green grass grows all around, all around
and the green grass grows all around.

LUXURY IS CULTURE AND NATURE

Culture, nature: the two rubbed against each other
until the arc of life was created.

Culture releases nature from its natural moderation, letting babel =
towers grow, letting spires become redder and redder, lavishly
while I dream of escaping this

complex being with bridges and passages
transporting bodies around
increasingly fleeting and flexible patterns

I long for life to reveal itself to me, in all its simplicity
without luxury and infrastructure, without machismo and institutions
nature washes through

castles
towers
you
me

with excessive force. Culture is superfluous = luxury.

Culture is a vital obstacle for nature = ivory. It drains
the foundation so

I
you
towers
castles

have a base to stand on. Culture is necessary = nature is a luxury
humans cannot afford.

Culture, nature: the two continue rubbing.

MY DISTANT INTERIOR

Time does not heal all:
when I was a wounded animal
I'd run into my distant interior and
perform the necessary mercy-killings myself.
Then I'd gather the bones on skin and
resurrect by sunrise in RED radiance.

In this way, *no one/nothing* has ever hurt *me*;
I remain unwritten.

The idea of exits with no openings, it must be chemically possible.
I dream of this: safety, no one coming in, nothing flowing.

That's the dream. It gets so lonely and cold in my arteries at night.

Another possibility: every hole seals itself and nobody leaves.
Once in my arteries you will stay inside forever.

I will make you become someone you hate being.

No one can make me admit to anything.

I'm driving by in my fuck-you wagon
exposing the shameful state of things:
the well in the forehead

what can I cover it with?

I'm driving by again
with something to cover it
a new language
a new pacifier.

The goal is to be infinite: no one will disagree with me, nobody can disagree with me.

To exist without form: no one will disagree with me, nobody can, none.

To be limitless: no one will disagree with me, nobody can, none, I am everything and everyone.

I have no hands but you can still
get fucked.

The idea that God is dead doesn't make me divine.

God's death necessitates I search for infinity elsewhere.

God's death will not bring me GLORIA.

God's death robs me the opportunity to become one.

I am no subject.

I have no characteristics.

I have no feelings.

Perhaps I'm hard to define, even to my
self, but at least I'm less sensitive to the loneliness
that everyone (everyone else) is subject to.

That's how great I am: my pain has nothing to do with me.

The goal is to ignore any kind of pain. The goal is that you, my loved ones,
will be able to ignore any kind of pain. Nobody, no one, will ever harm you,
not because they won't try, but because you will
be numb: open *vessels for coma*.

I refuse to cry; tears have no desire to leave.

The goal is to be the violator rather than be the victim.

The goal is mental, physical and existential numbness.
The cost is mute jubilation.

No one can make me say:
I am afraid.
Nobody
no one.

No one else can talk about my feelings. No one.

In order to feel like someone, eliminate the guilt of not being everyone.

I am everyone (that is closeness), I have to be everyone.

The goal is to not be afraid when someone breaks the bones in my right hand with a car door.

To be the evil one and never afraid.

The goal is for nothing to be expelled, neither the human nor its twin
(sack over the head), human.

The goal is for emptiness to be carried. Perhaps the goal is for emptiness to
be divided into smaller parts and carried over the arc of life, one part at a time;
for each of my loved ones to carry a vessel of mine. Perhaps I'll
carry a vessel of theirs, yours, one vessel from each. I'd like that.

The goal is to not be afraid when someone pushes me into a car and pulls
a sack over my head.

And I become whose twin?

The goal is for my offspring to be ruthless, brutal and fearless
for my offspring to come out of any situation as a conqueror.

All selection is natural.
Nature leads to all places. Nowhere.

The intersubjective: the closest one gets to another and
the farthest. We are uniform as the reflections of each other
but as mirrors no one knows the depths of others.

The goal is to not want anything from you.

The goal is to be immune, so that when a soft, warm hand strokes my neck to make the human flow, nothing will happen.

The goal is to not be afraid when someone puts out cigarettes on my skin.

I am against touching.

Do not try to stick
your hand through
my hatch.

The desire for no evil to make a difference.
The desire for every evil to be insignificant.

The desire for

*every hindrance, necessity, sternness, disregard, cynicism,
apathy, lack of self-control*

to be insignificant.

The goal is for no animal in the woods to smell my loss, smell my defeat.

The goal is for RED to be smelled by no animal in the woods.

e.g.

for no bush to be smelled in the garden
for no nest to be smelled in the bush
for no egg to be smelled in the nest
for no green grass to be smelled in the egg
and also not death.

The goal is to weaken every trace of odor. It will cost me my victory scent.

The goal is for my pain to be a phantom, for nothing real to have caused it: that's the only realistic painkiller available.

I believe in lukewarm human nature. No. I believe in cold human nature.

Refusing to be a victim is failing to see supremacy
for what it is: supremacy. The goal, deliver the victim as polished and
hog-tied as possible to my distant interior. Where no one can smell it.

If I'm being buried alive, why would I try to stay
calm? Someone might hear my panic and rejoice.

The goal is to do the work of suppression while you're caressing my
body.

Is the goal to do the work of suppression even while you're caressing
my body?

The goal is for my fear to be smelled by no one.

During my torture, I will sing
it will keep them out: as I walked

out, I dreamt a dream. What's unreal about me
must be perfectly clear, a midsummer's morning
bright, a dream last night

luminous.

Nothing can reach me.

The will to have no openings, to have no areas where humiliation and assault can take place.

Same for the bloodstream: no infrastructure
sun and moon chariots wheel at the slightest external touch
transporting bright shining humiliations within the corpus and
abracadabra out into every screaming corner.

I use expensive drops: anger's sweat, tablet, pastille, ointment. Balm. Brew three bags for a pot of coma.

With a rock I block the cave's mouth; nobody coming out, nobody coming in, nothing will resurrect, that name, that knife in the back will

never again slip through *my* paranoia-carcass.
I *will* remain unwritten.

The organ is either victim or conqueror in the system concerned.

The title is either fly or spider in the web concerned.

The act of killing could bring me even closer to my enemies
than the act of sex. That is to say: killing
them is the last thing I'd want to do.

A contradiction between means and end: I could desire to kill
my enemies, I mean, want them to not exist; but the appalling
idea of being closer to them discourages me.

A predatory instinct, turned on by life.
A predatory instinct, turned on by dying breath.
A predatory instinct, turned on by death.

The idea of two people growing so far apart that it's
impossible for both to remain human. Only if your self-loathing is real
can we meet in

the country of countless voices
the country without a middle
the country of infinite love.

Do not jump at your first opportunity to
misunderstand me if you want my friendship.

I am the one who hates displaying fear
no one can make me, I won't do it,

there is nothing in the world
there is nothing in the world that hurts me
there is nothing in the world I fear
there is nothing in the world as quiet as this
there is nothing in the world as quiet as this
there is nothing in the world as quiet as this.

No one can make me stop lying.

The goal is for my screams to work in mysterious waves
so no one can predict when, nobody can establish a sense of cause and
effect. No one should affect the pattern of my screams.

I am in comajubilation: no feeling can reach me here.

The goal is to cover any lukewarmness, cowardice, routine
with images of destruction.

Enter natural evil.
Enter natural sadism.

To conquer pain, to secure victory: that is the goal. To turn my body into stone and metal, cleave it in two and place both bodies in their true positions, pointing east and pointing west; bind them with strings of gold and steel to the arc of life. That is the goal.

Everything seems to have been snatched out of my body.

This is my new body language.

REALITY IS TANGIBLE AND INTANGIBLE

It continues, until tangibility breeds intangibility.
A lustful relationship with efficiency, productivity
makes reality solid, calculable, indivisible
as things become intangible
flowing in and out of

me
you
castles
towers
spires.

THESE MY CONTACT AREAS

The goal is: never having to confide in anyone. It's the same as never feeling the urge to write a word.

The idea that this goal is false.

The hope that this goal is false.

The idea that it's an advantage to know what you wish to destroy.

I.

The idea that it's a disadvantage to know what you wish to destroy.

I
you
castles
towers
spires.

The idea that it's a disadvantage to love what you wish to control.

The idea that it's an advantage to love what you wish to control.

The hope that
the hope that.

The idea that my coagulation can be shared with others.

The idea that this longing for numbness is
false after all.

The hope that this longing for numbness is false
after all.

A gift that doesn't demand a counter-gift.

An utterance that doesn't demand an answer.

We are limitless.

The goal is for my face to present the features: the eyes, the nose, the mouth, to bring them into the spotlight; and perhaps for the hair to lead the face.

The goal is to not be there as myself, but as spiderwebs: something that we all are, something we can give as a gift, like honey, via proboscis.

I can imagine you, even though you aren't here.
I can imagine you, even though I haven't seen you yet.

That is the structure.

I can imagine you, even though you'll never exist.

That is the structure, continued.

I spread out my territory, spiderweb/utopia
so it can lie like an

area of contact
and become limitless.

The goal is for an utterance to not demand an answer: a utopia inserted between the divided parts of the existing void.

Once there, all vessels will be connected.

I AM LIMITED AND UNLIMITED

Outwardly, my hands are
limited: five fingers, standard area of contact.

I didn't have a secret space, I just drew one; my residence
somewhere, a small castle made of bricks. In there, I took
necessary action without bringing into the heart
anything that cannot (must not) be there.

Internally, they are unlimited: at the end of each fingertip sits a new hand
all over, until my area of contact becomes limitless
until closeness = closeness.

My hands are internally/outwardly following the light, until
screen = area of contact = screen; one is an infinite
blank surface, the other a fractal abyss. Then I can tell how it feels
to have the world move over my outstretched hands
with its green, blue and yellow dreams. I wash
my contact areas in the moon after each encounter.

DARLING GLORIA

First we are connected, the way

you are inside me.

We are connected, but we haven't
met; they call it the big picture, which is

the heaviest DARLING to bear. I am only exposing
the structure.

Then we are separated, and they call it the big picture
a castle sinking into rubble.

As if we're the same at first; we're not.

As if things weren't already in rubble.

You are inside me like

I am the entire world, the fruit
in the garden: I am warmth, shelter, food
and transportation.

Then we are separated before we can meet
we are connected, then we separate.
In order to meet.

I am everything you are: I am warmth, shelter, food.

You were inside me
I was in the house
the house was by the lake
the lake was in the city
the city was in
inside the world.

I am everything
you are
I am warmth, shelter, food.

You ascend
to drink from sun and moon.

Before, I would have dreamt of a weapon
to kill the enemy; now I need a gun to shoot
you, before anyone harms a hair on your head.

The way

I am the house, you are inside me
as if I were a house.

The way

I am the castle, yes, I am
sinking into rubble, I won't be doing that
I just gained my towers, after all.

I am. God is the lifting of differences between part and whole.
The structure of breastfeeding is divine, we are God, every day

GLORIA.

Every hour there's milk that
hasn't seen the light of day
like the babel and ivory

that it is.

I am everything yet no one. This is
what I have exposed: you are

DARLING.

I have always existed in rubble. Only now did I
become a castle, after gaining my towers.

You must be separated before you can meet. That is the structure.

I call you

sweet pea
butterbean.

Those who transgress culture are essentially
founding it. I am. This place is too
high-ceilinged, big cathedral.

Idyllic and solemn.
Lonely and intimate.

Culture's footing continues, continues
to run away from culture.

They rub against each other:
thus fire was created.

Separation is required before we can meet, and we
have to meet. Mammals are based on this
transcendence-producing double movement.

Building and building
idyllic and solemn.
Building and building
lonely. And intimate.

Two towers, babel and ivory
are overflowing with groundwater/groundwine through culture.

We rub against each other: thus fire is created every day.

The overflow is running down the cradle of culture, through
the sheets: that's groundwater/groundwine, babel

ivory.

I am not telling anyone how to feel.

We must be separated before we can see each other
we must be separated before we can meet

that is the structure.

We have to die before we can meet. Before we can meet in all our
GLORIA.

That is the structure, continued.

DARLING, you make me think of
death every day.

The foundation did not breed culture and culture
did not lie down on top of the foundation

the area of contact seems limitless: the two
rub against each other, even if the area is no bigger

than a hand.

Overflow. Nature ran out
the cradle of culture and wet the sheets.
Inevitable. By chance, the two
were together the whole time:
two directions in the same cell, they

rubbed against each other, it rubbed off.

Should I connect with others, or should I exactly
not connect with others?

No contact area should go to waste.

Cradle

Wish, that the breast could grow around every hindrance,
necessity, sternness, disregard, cynicism, apathy, lack of
self-control, like a DELTA, DARLING, that any laceration of the
breast were insignificant. Because the chest was
without beginning or end.

I am the cradle of culture: throw yourself out from my towers.

You must cradle between these
members of one body.

Cradle between night and day, fall
between the towers.

Cradle between everyone and no one, members
of one body, birds and bees, cradle

between mussels and grains of sand, cradle
cradle between them.

Your life does not mean the same to you as it does to me.
My life does not mean the same to me as it does to you.
Our lives do not mean the same to any of us, everything is
systematic. I am the cradle of culture: lean, lean

out of my towers.

See it all.

Separation and the subsequent
union are terrifying. Necessary separation
and necessary union: a wall for
loneliness to irradiate.

This is GLORIA. I am holding you:
cradle, cradle.

Before I would have thrown myself over the arc of life; now I will catch you in
countless new ways.

I throw you up against the sky and
catch you as you fall. I am the
heavenmechanic. I am the world:
the fence and the sky in the garden. That is
what I am, all of it.
Everything.

My hands are becoming
spiderwebs: they adapt to what is held in them.

At the end of each fingertip is a new hand
which, at the end of each fingertip has a new hand
which, at the end of each fingertip has a new hand
which, at the end of each fingertip has a

cradle, so I can hold you
infinitely. My area of contact will become limitless.

You are my

foreign body

named body
fabled body
cradled body.

If your death is meaningless, it must be because you
are meaning, and losing you would be the loss of meaning
inside my distant interior: where meaning runs out, where
rose and name run
out.

My urine has smelled abnormally bitter the last few days.

The cradle, cradle of nature: I am not telling anyone how to feel
just telling it like it is. I am exposing the structure.

The facts are the
thin covers between
tenderness and transgression, every

feeling of culture.

Culture rises, nature rises
up and run out the crown of culture. They rub against each other: the towers
were there from the beginning, the crown of
culture, its builders and builders are its

cradle.Cradle.

I am singing GLORIA, I
am seeing the light of day.

DARLING, you are like feeding
a little bird by hand: I do not
know you. You are like a little bird. In a hand.

No, no, birds are not wild, they are free, free
while others are savage.

I do not know you: you are, I am, everything, look
look, you are smiling, and you can make anything
everything smile. It's running down your chin.

Building

You want to reach the top of the tower and learn
to enjoy the view, let it dislodge your despair with its

spires.

You are standing in the flood of survival
overflow, it's streaming down your chin.

The view spells
the birth of towers in your delicate heart. First you find your way
up: it exists in you and outside of you, a bent towards
stairs, erecting stairs, building bridges and passages.

The towers are there already; you need to
build the bridges, stairs. Remember, the towers are the cradle, cradle
of culture. Warm towers. Proud. You need to build a
complex being with bridges and passages
transporting bodies around
increasingly fleeting and flexible patterns

around the overflow of means, of social control
to be a society-suckling, political mammal.

There will be stairs and bridges and passages; there will be
tunnels, railings, pillars, vaults and there will be
stairs; there are houses, palaces, roads and
streets, and there have always

always been spires. Red spires.

You were inside me like I was a house; that does not
mean I know what's going on inside you. A house
does not know the interior of its resident.

That is the other wall for loneliness.
To irradiate.

My x-ray/loneliness.
Your loneliness/grass.

If you are to be tortured, I must
teach you to sing: as I walked out one midsummer's morning
it will keep them out.

You make me think, as I walked out, I must learn to sing
double with one voice,

whose song will fan into seven voices
whose songs will each fan into seven voices
whose songs will each fan into seven voices, whose songs will

make the air solid and prevent any movement. No one can move.
No one can harm you.

Hearts expand on closer inspection, that is to say
they dissipate.

Each chamber consists of four chambers
that each consist of four chambers
that each consist of four chambers
that each consist.

Is anything in there:

behind the treasury is a chestnut forest
behind the forest is a giant grin
behind the grin are the slippery, slippery floors
behind the floors is a small bowl of porridge
behind the bowl

neither emptiness nor wholeness is
found. Two walls for loneliness, only two.

This place is high-ceilinged. Big cathedral,
damp sheets, I am exposing.
The structure.

Loneliness, which is not connected to
freedom. Loneliness, which is still nothing
but savage.

Your loneliness is being created. Mine only has
two walls left.

I see you, behind the

bowl
floors
grin
forest
treasury

with a rolled-back eye, on the wing/x-ray:
a small skeleton.

Is what I see abandonment, or is it your budding
loneliness, your growing me-grass
your grass-you?

Rod.

You let the doctor stick
a needle in you, only because I'm holding you.

You let yourself be comforted
I could destroy you
you would have to trust me.

But the refining of loneliness has begun, it's going to be a
castle; it will become your castle that
can later gain two towers, can later lose one,
two walls.

There, there.
There, there, there. Silk and cream.
Forget about the red running in
herds under the silk through
cream.

Your smile comes running at me like a
herd down a hill, milk down the chin.

You make me think of death.

I wish that you could grow around every hindrance, necessity,
sternness, disregard, cynicism, apathy, lack of self-control
like a DELTA, DARLING, that any laceration of you were
insignificant. Because you were without beginning or end
because you are without capital, castle, throne. Ventricle.

You are the heart of us
we are the heart of the house
the house is the heart of the lake
the lake is the heart of the city
the city is the heart,
heart of the world.

It cradles.

Builds.

The selfishness of motherhood is
an ornament or a necessity, doesn't matter.

Your loneliness reaches around me
my loneliness reaches around the house
the loneliness of the house reaches around the lake
the loneliness of the lake reaches around the city
the loneliness of the city reaches around

the idea of being a society-suckling, political mammal.

As if birds would ever need gods
they are
gods themselves: delicate, lightweight gods with hollow bones
perched in gardens.

In all their GLORIA.

Possibilities:

I am a cocoon, you are my butterfly
I am namedrunk, you are nameless, (you must bloom)
I am nameless, you are namedrunk, (you must bloom)
I am a mussel, you are the pearl
I am a mussel, you are the pearl
I have become a castle, you will be

I am the cradle of culture
all day, every day.

From now on I will always be

atrium, ventricle, cubicle
complex being.

LIFE IS CHAOS AND ORDER

Life = the organized life of organisms = order.

Death = cessation of the organized life of organisms = cessation of order = chaos.

Life = growth = the struggle for survival between organisms = conflict = chaos.

Death = cessation of the struggle for survival = cessation of conflict = order.

()

Life = the organized life of organisms = order = freedom.

Death = cessation of the organized life of organisms = cessation of order = chaos = unfreedom.

Life = growth = the struggle for survival between organisms = conflict = chaos = unfreedom.

Death = cessation of the struggle for survival = cessation of conflict = order = freedom.

()

Life = the organized life of organisms = order = unfreedom.

Death = cessation of the organized life of organisms = cessation of order = chaos = freedom.

Life = growth = the struggle for survival between organisms = conflict = chaos = freedom.

Death = cessation of the struggle for survival = cessation of conflict = order = unfreedom.

To become more.

To become thick and RED and nutrient-rich; to lay
down and make deposits.

That is my new body language.

Why should I squirt semen when I can lay eggs?

I want more.

To collect semen from as many men as possible, when I am
RED and ready for reproduction. When you hit my sex, you are no one.

To have subversive lust components in my
distant interior.

I want more than just you. None of you awaken my dreams of
fusion: your sperm does. What I can become pregnant with does. All that
a human can become pregnant with does.

Get out of your stalls: I will hitch you to everything's wagon, I will ride you like
a charging bulldog, we will ride

straight up into

castles
towers
spires.

I want more than just love:
that's why I sucked dick
that night at Enghave Square.

All that a human can be pregnant with.

I am allowed more.

I am allowed to eat everything, all of you, as long as I
save the bones and pile them on your respective
skins after the meal.

My sex comprises what's there and what's not; that's why my sex is like the world.

What's not there makes my sex more fleshy, a paradox, jubilation, with its silence.

When you hit the spot. When you liberate yours.

You want to enter *my* paradise/spaceship where you think you can survive for several thousand years.

I want more.

To culture edifying lust components in my
distant interior.

You all dream of freedom
it's simple
liberate your cocks in me.

You search my name and get 20,000 tits.

Good tits
and bad tits.

20,000.

I want to be more.

Only an unfertilized egg can stay whole.

Every split kingdom is a wasteland.

I want to be every split kingdom:
gain twice the towers.

I want more than just love: I want

to become an army, become water

I

must penetrate everything.

I want what I am pregnant with, all that
a human can be pregnant with

to become an army, become water
to traverse the world

to penetrate everything.

That is my new body language.

DYNAMIC IS FEMALE AND MALE

The male and the female, I rub these two against each other
until everything happens, I think with babel cunt, with ivory brain
until I think with babel brain, with ivory cock, and nothing inside
me will keep you from going there, where society is not, and color
your longings with RED radiance.

You are male = dynamic = moveable = soft.

I am female = static = hard.

You are male = stiff = static.

I am female = flexible = plastic = dynamic.

Anything is possible.

My invisible servants are massaging, massaging the coast of
life, and everything wavers.

Here
it flows.

Here, everyone
makes someone else's money.
That is the exposed structure.

Transactions with no voice.
Transactions with two tongues.
Transactions with eternal life.

I am massaging society.
I massage, or the elements won't function.
I massage and

plankton runs through
money runs through
loneliness runs through society

in the third millennium.

The loneliness of plankton dissolved in
the whale's loneliness dissolved in
human loneliness dissolved in

I am Harmless: my transactions are already countless.

I send reality out to sea, I have already sent reality out to sea
but before the sea sends reality back to me
it sends reality to those on the floor below me
and before that
it sends reality to those on the floor
below those on the floor below me
and before that
it sends reality to those on the floor
below those on the floor below
those living below me.

Will this strengthen or weaken the human sense of smell?

First, the bill is paid by someone whose destructions can be overlooked
then, the bill is paid by someone whose destructions can be counted

when the bill reaches me, it can be overlooked, the opportunity
for future destruction won't be hindered. I frolick
on the arc of life.

I want to buy my way to everything: I want to buy my way to
ruthlessness, a triumphal wagon,
a vault over reality

and pale balm in the end.

If I want a taste of ecstasy without losing myself, then I must lose
something else, must lose something else.

I am losing *you* behind *my* wagon.

Things do not lose their spirit by being commodities: they lose firmness, transform into sources, their own sources, the origin of things; after that, everything is pure flow running through society like lemmings, like

desires with two tongues
desires with double lives
desires with eternal love.

All desires are false desires, paradoxes, jubilation, a surplus that starts to flow when you, I, come into mouthservice and culture's yellow, blue and green dreams light up in their squares.

All animals in the forest can smell the cashflow
all animals in the forest can smell the flow of languages
all animals in the forest can smell the food chains.

Truth and justice, I want to cut
their hearts out
carefully, and use them as earrings; I'll be all dressed up.

I'll run out on the arc of life and buy my way into luxury.

I have to be
innocent, blind, nobody; no
reality will penetrate my eyes.

No one will stream through *my* paranoia-carcass.

Shipments from hand to mouth are
mouthservices, my invisible servants, nothing is
wrong with what they offer.

I wipe *my* face in
their sweat-embroidery.

I want my original cruelty back;
I will take Mother Market's lead
and play tricks on dynamic individuals in the midst of desert and
forest.

We must go out and knock old ladies down, should we start with
me? I want to knock old ladies down, I will start with me.

I'm punching as hard as I can while covering my ears.

I sink my teeth as I please into
desert and forest.

I won't feel sorry for you when you don't get yours, I will rejoice
my new ruthlessness.

If I am for a multicultural society, then I will be raped by
strange men; if I am for a monocultural society, then I will
be raped by familiar men. I must choose the names
of those I want to be penetrated by against my will.

Everyone must choose the name of what will flow
through them. Against their will. Ideally. RED or GLORIA.
All my breast buddies are freezing.

Rationality will not save us; chlorine
will. A big batch of chlorine spilled over

complex being with bridges and passages.

I have let reality into my heart where it paints with
RED.

Paradise, where everyone is penetrated by me
paradise, where no one is penetrated by anything
paradise, where everyone is penetrated by everything
paradise, where I am penetrated by everyone.

Your money up in *my* ass.

Joyful Capitalism I
In the original gift economies, *humans, animals,*
jewelry, food, land, gods, work, status, were elements included in the
exchange. Now, only those sold through human trafficking are sold
by others; aside from that, everyone here is selling themselves. With gratitude.
Credibility is, naturally, the most important product on my shelves.

Joyful Capitalism II
It is a greater pleasure to penetrate a virgin market.
When the market is female, the individuals, who are cocks, will dream of
it in all its virginity: the dream of a virgin market, the dream of an untouched
market, which the first cock will believe it has conquered. That is the universal
symbol of a liberal economy. Even though the market will always be
the mother: open and powerful.

Joyful Capitalism III
I will say this about world peace: eventually, when everyone is fat and content
like me, it will come. It will be big and lazy.

Joyful Capitalism IV
Here, everyone makes someone else's money. That is the exposed structure.

Joyful Capitalism V
Here, everyone pays the bill for others, paradox, orbit, with
their lives.

The dream of living off flowers and dew
of only eating bodies without infrastructure, institutions.

The dream of being invulnerable
of not personally having infrastructure, institutions.

Prissy, prissy dreams;
they have dug *their* chambers
in *my* paranoia-carcass.

Am I not standing here like a
risk-willing vessel?

I am significant: I destroy the world.

If you've ever sold anything to anyone, i.e. art, i.e. on a stage, then you are a whore/woman and a victim in the patriarchal order. Thus, everyone in this society is a woman: that's what a feminized society means. All individuals are still dicks in relation to Mother Market. In this society everyone is a woman with a dick.

The fact that every: you can be bought, is a humiliation,
every: you are for sale, is a humiliation. You can
always smell them, even though everyone here
sells themselves. With gratitude.

I am a rocking horse. Hitch me to your wagon.

One reality is slaughtered at another reality's altar
the other reality is slaughtered at the third reality's altar
the third reality is slaughtered at the fourth's and

humans, animals, gods
work, loneliness
babel and ivory

stream from hand to mouth, from

one's hand to the other's mouth
the other's mouth to the third's

my servants, my invisible servants are
an army, they take my soul, must become water
must traverse everything while singing GLORIA;

all realities must be avenged, each and every one.

I want my original cruelty back;
then I will take Mother Market's lead
and force flexible and dynamic individuals to
massage me right in the third-millennium heart.

Together, we will beat
in the great DELTA.

I feed the birds. They don't like that
so many others are looking
to be corrupted by me.

Personally, I don't care:
eat from my hand, today's
mouthservice, I am your

sugar mama
sugar brother
sugar daddy
sister

what do I know, it's all the same, my invisible servants:

sweat mama
sweat brother
sweat daddy
sweat sister

what do I know, *I* ornament myself with *their* food chains.

I am a flexible individual balancing my power, making friends with
the underpinnings, my rib cage is collapsible.

I am the dynamic individual: I am a dickhead, for crying out loud
my social criticism is swelling more than I am, just look, it's
purpleblue now, for fucks sake, purpleblue, purpleblue, purpleblue.
I call myself man, woman, victim, wise-ass, but really I'm just a dickhead.
My social criticism is a tribute to purpleblue, my product is elastic.

The heat takes up too much space, no room for pity, all transactions
stream through the channels, hot NEWS, the perfect temperature for
bathing.

Heavy is the head that the crown wears
into desert or forest.
With three LULLABIES clamping down the neck.
A moon chariot follows with blindness and solace, at last,
one crown, two crowns, three crowns, four crowns, lubricating with
five crowns' worth of pale balm over the body.

And then there's me, sitting on the couch:
I don't dance, travel, or hunt; I'm good at thinking, but I
have a guilty conscience.

The Matriarchate I
If the market is a mother, then it must be milked.
If the individual is a cock, then it must use a condom.

The Matriarchate II
If a rich man can be milked, then he is a mother.

The Matriarchate III
You can fuck Mother Market, it won't help anything.
Every hole seals itself.

The Matriarchate IV
Dynamic and flexible individuals are both stretched between a Big
Mother State and the dream of a virgin market.

The Matriarchate V
Choose between a Big Mother State and a Big Mother's Darling Boy State.

Is there anyone else who would like to be mocked by me?

I drive around to people with empty
vessels and collect money.

I drive around in my me-wagon and peddle
these my contact areas

and I will get paid.

The customer is fucked, that's the new truth, the truth
I have to sell

you. I feed
the birds, new truths, who fucking needs
them, I feed the birds.

Mother Market's lover-me-lover-me-not dances with the food
chains of the world in its hair.

My invisible servants, their hearts I know like my own, the third-millennium's, DELTA of starvation and oversaturation.

My servants, my invisible servants, their clusterhearts are beating against the coast of life.

Only Mother Market displays such mercy: she says:

Dance in your
15-minute temple

sell your used goods
play your old solo
now.

No movement can be wasted.

I massage, and reality penetrates my heart.
I massage, and my heart separates from reality again.

The dynamic individual
fucks the flexible individual at the center of
the arc of life.

The sun hires its servants
personally; I don't see mine.
I don't test the sharpness of their teeth:
their situation is not my problem.

Mother Market is the feminine's final victory,
together with her, I will whisper: be calm

little child of time;
I am increasing productivity for you, increasing.

Consider this an egoism-exorcism, always fascinated by selfishness itself, hence the necessity for a ceremony with selfishness and my me-wagon, in shiny velvet leading the holy procession.

STATE IS FATHER AND MOTHER

State = father = lawfulness = civilization vs. nature = mother = freedom = subversive.

Father = individual = cock = subversiveness vs. lawfulness = collective = mother = state.

I drive among you, pregnant with what I am pregnant with, in through the town gate; I let it out into the night, what's inside me, it walks among you, right there among you.

I tell the herd of all things:
Whatever you're smeared in, I will wash it off
and wrap you in what I have

and cradle.

I lift the names off the foreheads of all things
I carry them away in the belly of the fish
plant a tree.

This is the new name, letting interior and exterior meet
from root to crown.
At last.

Forehead pointing west, a woman sits
and between her legs, another woman sits, forehead
pointing west
and between the other woman's legs, a third woman sits, forehead
pointing west
and between the third woman's legs

the new sun rises.

Pate pointing east, a man sits on knees and hands
and above him, pate pointing east, another man curls on
knees and hands
and above him, pate pointing east, a third man curls on
knees and hands
and above

above him the new sun sets.

In this marble heaven/hell, the mother causes chains of men to not know they miss each other, and chains of women to not know what they are missing.

And all blood is equally old; only our hearts become newer and newer catacombs.

Everything must stream through *my* paranoia-carcass.

I'm telling it like it is, when reality moves over the surface of
the heart, the third-millennium's = 40 inches transporting images of

complex being with bridges and passages
transporting bodies around
increasingly fleeting and flexible patterns

around increasingly fleeting and flexible patterns, under the new sun, over
the irony of the sea.

There is a need for new temples, new pillars to keep
the roof from falling down on
atrium, ventricle, cubicle, falling down on

complex being.

At the end of each tree in the fuck-forest are seven branches
and, at the end of each are seven smaller branches
and, at the end of each are seven leaves
and, at the end of each are seven points
and, at the end of each is the

desert of many voices
desert of multiple yellow eyes
desert of eternal love.

The empty heart/land is just as unpredictable as others: it flows
when wind massages the sand.

Not the individual

*"Le monde occidental est perverti. Pas les individus. La culture est
pervertie, pas l'individu."*
(Hawad)

The individual and the entire tissue

Are the larger structures fayed into the individual *en miniature*, or is
only the tissue itself perverted? Does the entire tissue,

the entire city with falling towers exist
inside me,
and if that exists,
do all the castles and skies, tied to spires with strings of
gold and steel, exist to force the tissue to collaborate with the air in a
dome-shaped unit, hanging by long threads from the sky
inside me,
and if that exists,
does the entire spiderweb planet, sending winces from every point of the
surface to every other point of the surface and down, exist,
no one escapes
inside me,
and if that exists,

do I exist
inside myself?

In there, I move through the most common
of riddles.

Not the individual

Every day actions, with consequences that cannot (must), cannot (must)
stay inside the heartspace: a flat screen displaying images
invented by no one, no more space
only pixel.

The heart must rise up to the over-exposed reality,
must be stretched out and tied up with strings of gold
between the distant interior and the arc of life.

That is the new contact area.

A new screen for culture's yellow, blue and
green dreams to move past.

The individual and the entire tissue

The idea that the entire spiderweb, the entire rhythm, all, nothing, is something that has been preinstalled on the inside, *en miniature*. I dreamt that I saw a hatchling in someone's hand, not mine, but I know that

I exist,
inside the heart of the hatchling,
and if I exist,
so does the entire city with falling towers
inside the heart of the hatchling,
and if that exists,
so do all the castles and skies, tied to spires with strings of
gold and steel, in order to force the tissue to collaborate with the air in a
dome-shaped unit, hanging by long threads from the sky
inside the heart of the hatchling,
and if that exist,
so does the entire spiderweb planet, sending winces from every point of the
surface to every other point of the surface and down,
no one escapes
inside the heart of the hatchling.

No one escapes.

Not the individual

I don't know if I belong, don't know if I can (must) be there.
I didn't have a secret space, I just drew one; my residence
somewhere, a small castle made of bricks. In there, I took
necessary action without bringing into the heart
anything that cannot (must not) be there

that cannot (must not) be there
that cannot (must not) be there.

The individual and the entire tissue

Individuals rush through culture, and culture rushes through
individuals; I've got

towers
castles
you
me

inside, *en miniature*. I feel them at night.

The spiderweb planet created when I rub my fingers against
each other
and the spiderweb planets created when everyone rubs everyone's
are uniform.

We hand each other planets and spiderwebs in caring and non-caring
tethered to larger and larger webs of caring and non-caring.

We catch fish, while life rides off
between our fingers.

Like women riding men.

You-wagon, something that drives across the cheeks in a distinctive, dancing fashion.

I-wagon, a bus with dead passengers waking up, one of whom sat next to me (without skin).

Society formation without middle
society formation without infrastructure
society formation without organs/institutions

I-wagon formation without middle
I-wagon formation without infrastructure
I-wagon formation without organs/institutions

you-wagon formation without middle
you-wagon formation without infrastructure
you-wagon formation without organs/institutions.

We use each other as something we are not, beat a new identity into each other's distant interior. Everything is massage.

We use the world as something it is not, beat a new identity out over exobrains, hearts, blood: it belongs to our enemies as well, everything unfolds like the name, the strident flag.
The universe is massage.

Nature's inherent unnature is born via heroic deed;
all overstatement, overflow, born via heroic deed;
plucked eyebrows and shiny machines, born via heroic deed;
forcing spiders to spin their webs over the portals of
change, born via heroic deed;
ideology's nine lives, born via heroic deed;
The great sparkler, death's peer, who throws up tales
born via heroic deed.
The irony of the sea is born. Sailing over the irony of the sea is born
via heroic deed.
My movement toward the sun's path toward death
is born via heroic deed.
Survival is a large-scale movement. A softness in the moon. Born via
heroic deed.
Machismo and luxury are origins and originally born via heroic deed.

It is impossible to distinguish between food bowl and decoration, between survival and ornament, luxury and life. New identity.

We fill our vessels with machismo, the original sentiment, and drown in the luxury of death.

I want to beat against the coast of life as hard as I can. I want, I want.

We must play our babelchords to culture: it will change
beyond recognition. Every void will be a

vessel for holy spirits and nightingales and

society's towers will grow into the sky, where we will tie them to
the arc of life with bands of steel: a decent apparatus
for the two, earth and sky, human and life, to,
for once in history, constitute a whole.

We roll the wild carpet of mute jubilation out over the world
like horses
like women riding men
coming out of nothing and riding back into nothing on the same
night, the next morning, like sun chariot and

moon chariot over the sky.

Surviving is essentially luxurious.

Your exoheart embraces me
my exoheart embraces the house
the exoheart of the house embraces the lake
the exoheart of the lake embraces the city
the exoheart of the city embraces
the world

that turns everyone into siblings.

I put all the little
orb-shaped worlds of glass back
in their cosmic framings, and everything becomes everything.

All must be one

First, I drown in the radiance of the world. Then, I want to be the opposite of
radiance: a dullness, hiding me and drawing everything to me, turning
all into one.

First, I open my limits to everything. Then, once I penetrate myself,
everyone, woman, man, babel and ivory,
will turn into me.

I want to gather it all, the world, myself, in one single
sex, like balm on my crown of unfertilized eggs.

When I have incubated the world in my heart valves and birthed it
from my womb and breasts like the animal kingdom and the Milky Way;
when it has consolidated into globes and stars and starts to shine, starts time,
then the struggle will enclose it, once again, like a womb, and
turn all into one. The womb of struggle.

I have tucked everything inside my rib cage, that's what it's there for, my war
chest. Soon I will press my breasts against reality, and everything will
come out in one squirt: all will point to one.

I want to drink all the world's juices and let my offspring drink me up
via breasts. I want to drink it all, let one drink all, via these
my bottomless drinking horns.

All must be one again

I will let myself be born out of everything, like expensive drops
running out of squashed things; I will let everything be
born out of me, everything that is snatched out of my body.

I will string myself up, bent in neon, like the arc of life,
and I will let the arc of life double up in pain
like me.

I have been through everything's stone grinder; now I send
everything out through my thresher. The sword
that the sheath is pregnant with: just wait until it is drawn.

I have let reality into my heart; now I will open reality's
hearts and place myself on all its thrones. I will be everywhere
at once.

I have had everything inside me; now I must enter everything, aided by
mightier types of penetration, like water, penetrating a flower's stem,
saturating the flower in its outermost fibers. All vessels are connected. All
must point to everything.

I will let all sexes come to me, and I want to be all
sexes; I am gruesome
and soft as velvet.

I will penetrate the sea like an arrow, and the sword I am
pregnant with will be pulled out of me like an army;
an army that must be like water, one and all.

One must be all

I fell from the tree's branches, like yellow leaves; In my womb, I must now plant a tree that will be the entire world.

But first: *I* create *you* from mother of pearl.

We are not moving towards the future; it comes rushing to us like
terrible NEWS, towers, like

atrium, ventricle, cubicle
complex being with bridges and passages
transporting bodies around
increasingly fleeting and flexible patterns

crashing down at the speed determined by law
from the sky.

That is the future.

Suppression and expectation move through my distant interior holding
each other's hands.

Reality is an overheating of facts, flowing NEWS, somebody will
keep an eye on the red-hot things,

and they will get paid.

Warmth, shelter, food. Transportation: I say my sun chariot and moon
chariot. We drive, they drive unborn lives out to the middle of the arc
of life and drop them off, without breath's temple, without any temple, nobody
says anything. They, we, drive through the sphinx-gate of breasts, without
a sound, and hang them under a sign that says: Every loss is a defeat. Light
never stands still. Ever. Transportation, I say: my sun chariot and moon
chariot. We drive out to hang everything under the new mommy-daddy-sun:
a vessel filled to overflowing.

I have withdrawn to my Tower of Babel; here, nothing
is the way it was just before. Everything flows.

I give away my third-millennium heart, I send it into orbit and get it
back tenfold, it grows via the babel effect

tenfold, tenfold, tenfold

so much

complex being

I'll never be able to get it back in, it's towering up, it's
pouring out over the arc of life, founding
my towers and cities.

In my towers and cities, all monuments must be hollow. Their blustering is
the tribute the world needs, prompted

not by stupidity, not by flatness, not by high or low morals
but by a true void

vessel of holy spirit and

I am not a soulfisherman, I am a sower: carrying around my me-coffin,
a box hanging upside down by threads, like bait from a fishing rod,
and lowering it into the human I meet on the way. A sower: trying
to reach the human, the distant interior, with my cheap seeds, via
fixtures and lowering mechanisms.

My shopping bags of fertilized eggs: the birds cannot, the wind cannot, no
one can carry them, spread them; they must hit the country's spot without
any help from the wind, from the birds.

If spring doesn't fail, if summer doesn't fail, if
fall doesn't fail, the harvester gets to work.

My life is hanging by long threads from the sky: a spindle apparatus that keeps it in place, in an upright position in my chest. When oceans rise in the throat, life's anchor is threatened.

The judge says *all rise*, and the big blue courtroom gets up and swallows

humans, animals, gods
or even hearts
complex beings

unless I pull the organs out of my rib cage, playpen, and
send them into orbit.

And so I get to sit here, my vital organs hovering around me like
a solar system; makes it easier to see them and keep an eye on them,
to unpack my summerheart and send it into orbit.

If spring doesn't fail.

It's easier to go get my coma-eggs and run my
verdigris-wagon, seed-wagon over the forehead with
deafness, blindness, namelessness, everything I've got, suppressed
information

that can soothe.

That's what we need.

Your LULLABY
over the wrath of *my* center.

What's on my heart tonight? Visions and hot NEWS
on my heart, yours; what can you watch on my reality heart? Tall, black
visions, like I showed you:

mothers with no voice
mothers with half faces
mothers with eternal love

towers with 1000 chambers
towers with yellow, blue and green eyes
towers with red, red spires

fathers with many voices
fathers with nine lives
fathers with gentle, gentle eyes.

Unborn lives mount up in the cradles of culture, nature and
lie still
stay quiet.

THE HEART IS CORE AND CITY

The divisible and the indivisible rub against each other at our center. We all
have third-millennium hearts, we need more time, we withdraw to our own
separate hearts; here, nothing is just like before, everything flows.
No difference between outside and inside, it's all heart, no
one needs to go out,

the tissue
castles
towers
you
I

exist inside me: I walk through myself via this tissue, via the heart,
institution, via

complex being with bridges and passages
transporting bodies around
increasingly fleeting and flexible patterns

until my heart is a city inside me that

humans, animals, gods
work, loneliness
babel and ivory

move through. And when I walk out among

castles
towers
spires

my heart becomes small, indivisible, like a core. In it, you can stick your sword
and plant your strident flag: your triumph on the battlefield.

I am not who I am.

I must be who I become.

ALL AND NO VESSELS ARE CONNECTED

TRANSLATOR'S NOTE

Ursula Andkjær Olsen is one of Denmark's most important contemporary poets. A poets' poet and a critics' darling, she won the prestigious literary award Montanaprisen in 2013 for her poetry collection *Det 3. årtusindes hjerte (Third-Millennium Heart)*, from a judging committee who hailed Olsen as "one of the wildest and sharpest intellects in Danish contemporary poetry." In 2017, Olsen received the Danish Arts Foundation's Award of Distinction with this statement from the committee: "Few poets, if any, have renewed Danish poetry in the 21st century the way Ursula Andkjær Olsen has done it."

When offered to translate this 214-page collection — Olsen's first book in English translation — I was both excited and terrified. In addition to frequently inventing new words and enjoying the occasional pun, Olsen is known for her many playful references to Danish idioms and songs, as well as Norse mythology, the Bible, philosophy, and science. The most difficult part of translating her poetry, however, has to do with Olsen's use of voice. The speaker in *Third-Millennium Heart* is an ambiguous character: abusive, yet a victim; fiercely emotional, yet icy and cynical. In *Kritik*, a Danish journal of scholarly art criticism, Ida Bencke addresses this complexity in her research article "The Body Is Something Else: Posthumanism and Cyborg Hearts in the Work of Ursula Andkjær Olsen":

> In *Third-Millennium Heart*, an utterly monstrous character of the body is presented to us: a heart, whose arteries and chambers lead us into complex architectural constructions and mythical castle facilities. From this hybrid body-space a terrifying female figure arises, spewing a long list of contradictory judgments and prophesies out over the Western world's perverted civilization and market mechanisms. The work is composed of several short, out-of-breath-like texts that aggressively branch out, pointing in wild and completely different directions. As a matter of fact, the ambiguity of this third-millennium heart character is so prevalent that any reading of its intentions could be disproved with an equally well-documented interpretation of the exact opposite statement.

This duality is possible in the original language because Danish grammar allows for multiple ideas — separated by a wet monsoon of commas — to (e)merge within a single sentence. To accommodate this duality in translation, I replaced some commas with line breaks, to entertain the possibility of connections between certain words or lines. In other cases, when a line break would cause more confusion than clarification, I inserted a colon or a period instead.

I also chose to break lines differently when the translated poems invited new possibilities for wordplay, or when I deemed an English line too clunky. In terms of Olsen's invented words, I had to come up with solutions on a case-by-case basis. At times, when the effect wasn't too awkward, I was able to translate these words directly. However, with words such as *væksthund* (growth-dog), I had to get creative in order to make the reference to capitalism slightly more apparent in translation. In this particular case, I ended up with "charging bulldog": a nod (or middle finger) to the Charging Bull on Wall Street, an American symbol of aggressive financial optimism and prosperity.

— Katrine Øgaard Jensen

Third-Millennium Heart by Ursula Andkjær Olsen
Translated from the Danish by Katrine Øgaard Jensen

© 2017 Ursula Andkjær Olsen, Broken Dimanche Press, and Action Books
Translation copyright © 2017 Katrine Øgaard Jensen

First published as *Det 3. årtusindes hjerte*
© 2012 Ursula Andkjær Olsen and Gyldendal, Copenhagen

ISBN 978-3-943196-45-0
Library of Congress Control Number: 2017944529

Editors: Ida Bencke, Joyelle McSweeney, Johannes Göransson
Cover Design: Sophia Kalkau

A co-publication between Broken Dimanche Press and Action Books

 ACTIONBOOKS

brokendimanche.eu
actionbooks.org

With the generous support from
DANISH ARTS FOUNDATION

Parts of this manuscript first appeared, in slightly different versions, in *Asymptote*,
Washington Square Review, *Denver Quarterly*, *Arc Poetry Magazine*, *Words without Borders*, and *The Scores*.